Contents

Let's Visit a Farm Community 4

Homes 6

Getting Around. 8

Schools 10

Working 12

Keeping Safe. 14

Shopping. 16

Food 18

Libraries. 20

Money and Mail. 22

Other Places in a Farm Community 24

Having Fun 26

The Farm Community Comes Together 28

Glossary 30

More Books to Read. 31

Index 32

Let's Visit a Farm Community

People everywhere live in **neighborhoods**.
A neighborhood is a small part of a larger
community, such as a city or town.
A neighborhood's people and places help
to make it special.

Neighborhood Walk

Farm Community

Peggy Pancella

Heinemann Library
Chicago, Illinois

© 2006 Heinemann Library
an imprint of Capstone Global Library
Chicago, Illinois

Visit our website at www.heinemannlibrary.com

Photo research by Jill Birschbach
Designed by Joanna Hinton-Malivoire and Q2A

Printed in the United States of America in Eau Claire, Wisconsin.
122014   008673RP

Library of Congress Cataloging-in-Publication Data
Pancella, Peggy.
  Farm community / Peggy Pancella.
    p. cm. -- (Neighborhood walk)
  Includes bibliographical references and index.
  ISBN 1-4034-6216-X (hc) -- ISBN 1-4034-6222-4 (pb)
  ISBN 978-1-4034-6216-9 (hc) -- ISBN 978-1-4034-6222-0 (pb)
  1. Sociology, Rural--Juvenile literature. 2. Farm life--Juvenile literature. I. Title. II. Series.
  HT421.P26 2006
  307.72--dc22
                                2005010648

Acknowledgments
The author and publisher are grateful to the following for permission to reproduce copyright material:
Corbis p. 25 (Tim Wright); Getty Images/Image Source p. 26; Heinemann Library pp. 4 (top & bottom, Jill Birschbach), 5 (top & bottom, Robert Lifson), 6 (Jill Birschbach), 7 (Jill Birschbach), 8 (Jill Birschbach), 9 (Jill Birschbach), 10 (Jill Birschbach), 11 (Jill Birschbach), 12 (Jill Birschbach), 13 (Greg Williams), 14 (Jill Birschbach), 15 (Scott Braut), 16 (Jill Birschbach), 17 (Jill Birschbach), 18 (Rudi Von Briel), 19 (Jill Birschbach), 20 (Jill Birschbach), 21 (Jill Birschbach), 22 (Jill Birschbach), 23 (Jill Birschbach), 24 (Jill Birschbach), 29 (Robert Hashimoto); Photo Edit, Inc. 27 (David Young-Wolff), 28 (Robert Brenner)

Cover photograph reproduced with the permission of Getty (Stone/Mitch Kezar)

Every effort has been made to contact copyright holders of any material reproduced in this book. Any omissions will be rectified in subsequent printings if notice is given to the publisher.

Some words are shown in bold, **like this**. You can find out what they mean by looking in the glossary.

Some neighborhoods are farm communities.
A farm community includes a small town and
the farms around it. There may be hundreds or
thousands of people. The people and places
are usually spread across a large area.

5

Homes

Some homes are near each other and others are far apart.

Farm **communities** have many kinds of homes. People who live on farms usually live in houses with lots of land all around. Some people live in houses closer to town. They often have large yards as well.

People in farm communities may also live in **mobile homes** or trailers. These homes are often set up in groups outside the town. In the town, many people live in apartments that are above stores.

Mobile homes can be moved but usually stay in one place.

Getting Around

Places in farm **communities** are usually spread out, so people often use cars to get around. Farm workers also use trucks, tractors, and horses.

A farm community's roads run past many fields.

Trains can carry many kinds of products at once.

In town, people often walk or ride bikes for short trips. Big trucks and trains may also travel through the town. They pick up **crops** and other farm products. They take these things to cities to be sold.

Schools

Schools in farm communities often have room for large play areas.

Farm **communities** have few people, so they need few schools. Sometimes there is only one school building for all of the students, from elementary school to high school.

Some farm communities do not have enough children to fill a school. They may share a school with a neighboring town. Some students have to travel far to get to school. They often ride on school buses or in cars.

Buses may pick up children who live far from the school.

Working

In farm **communities**, most jobs have to do with farming. Farmers grow **crops** and raise animals. Some workers sell farm machines and supplies. Others help farmers buy and sell their animals and crops.

Farmers use special machines to plant and pick their crops.

Some jobs must be done every day, such as milking cows.

There is a lot of work to do on farms. Even children may care for animals or help in the fields. Other people work at stores, restaurants, and businesses in the town. A few workers **commute** to jobs in bigger towns or in a nearby city.

Keeping Safe

Some workers in farm **communities** help keep people safe. A farm community usually has only a few police officers. They use cars to **patrol** the area because places are so spread out.

Police, fire, and emergency workers may share one station.

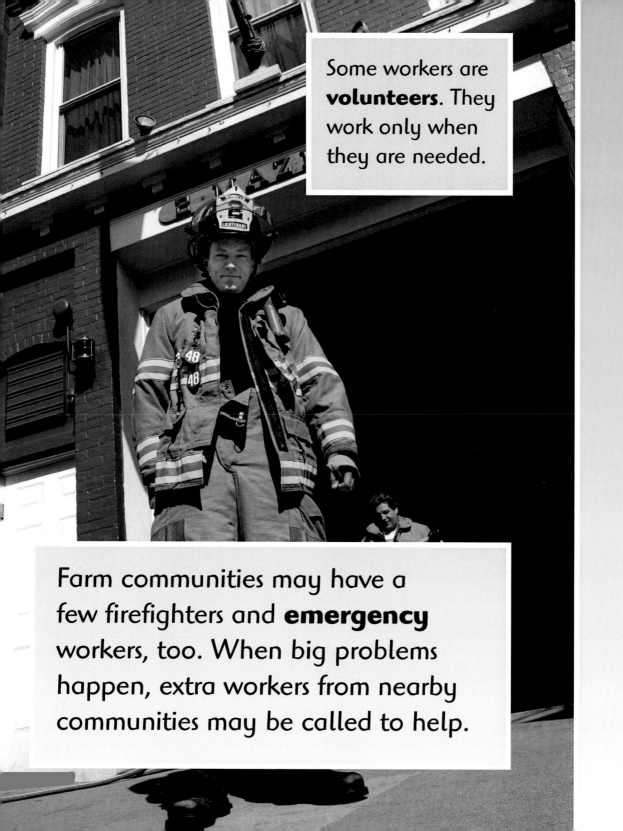

Some workers are **volunteers**. They work only when they are needed.

Farm communities may have a few firefighters and **emergency** workers, too. When big problems happen, extra workers from nearby communities may be called to help.

15

Shopping

Most of a farm **community's** stores are in the center of town. There is usually a **business district** along the main road. The small shops here sell clothes, farming supplies, and other items.

The business district includes all kinds of shops.

There is more room for larger stores outside the town.

There are sometimes other stores outside the town. Some large stores sell many kinds of products. People in farm communities sometimes have to visit bigger towns to find everything they need to buy.

Food

Farmers may set up stands to sell what they grow.

Many farmers grow fruits, vegetables, or grains. Some raise cows for milk or chickens for eggs. Others sell their animals to be used as food. These products feed people across the country and around the world.

Small grocery stores in town and larger supermarkets outside of town also sell food. The town usually has places to eat, too.

Farm communities often have a restaurant in the center of town.

Libraries

Some farm **communities** have their own libraries. Two or more neighboring communities may also share a library. Some towns do not have a library at all. They may have a **bookmobile** that brings them things to read.

Libraries in farm communities are usually small.

HUTCHINSON MEMORIAL LIBRARY

Librarians help people find books and information.

These libraries and bookmobiles often do not have very many books. They may borrow books from libraries in other towns. **Librarians** can also use computers to find out information that people need.

Money and Mail

ATMs make banking quick and easy.

A farm **community** may have only one or two banks. People may do business inside or use a drive-up window or **ATM**. Banks sometimes **lend** money to farmers so they can buy machines and supplies.

There is usually a post office in town, too. People can mail letters and packages or pick up their mail here. Letter carriers drive cars to deliver most of the mail because homes are often far apart.

Many people have their mailboxes at the side of the road.

Other Places in a Farm Community

A farm **community** has other important buildings, too. There may be a **town hall** where **government** leaders meet. There may also be churches, temples, and other places of worship.

Leaders make plans and rules for the farm community at the town hall.

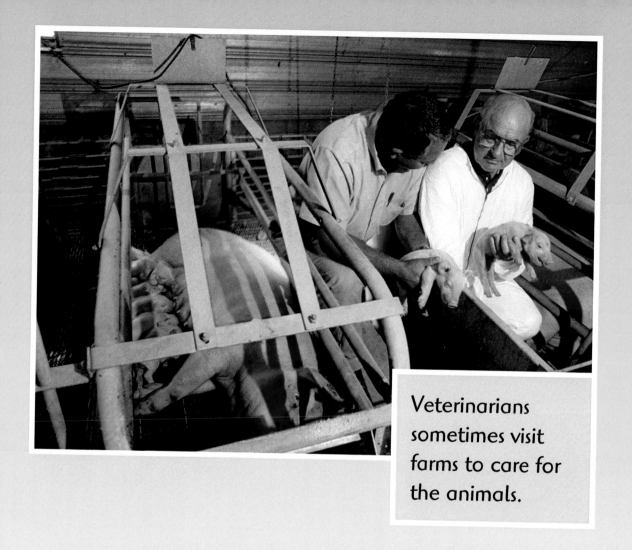

Veterinarians sometimes visit farms to care for the animals.

People who need care can visit a doctor's office. The nearest hospital is usually in a city or larger town. Most farm communities also have **veterinarians**. These doctors care for sick or hurt animals.

Having Fun

People in farm **communities** like to relax with their families and friends. Sometimes they play on their own farms. They may also enjoy outdoor activities like hunting, fishing, hiking, and horseback riding.

Many people enjoy fishing in lakes, ponds, and streams.

Some farm communities have their own sports teams.

There are often parks and ball fields in or near the town. Many towns also have theaters where people can watch movies or hear music concerts. People sometimes travel to the city for special activities, too.

27

The Farm Community Comes Together

The farm community stays strong when everyone pitches in.

People in farm **communities** often help each other. They may work together to pick **crops** or care for animals. They may also share food and other supplies with those in need.

Many farm communities hold fairs or **rodeos**.
People show their animals and sell things they
have grown or made. They share food, music,
games, and fun. All these things make farm
communities great places to live.

At a rodeo,
people show
how well they
can ride and
handle animals.

Glossary

ATM bank machine that people use to put in and take out money

bookmobile bus or van that brings library books to people in different places

business district area in the middle of a town where there are many businesses

community group of people who live in one area, or the area where they live

commute travel from home to work and back

crop food grown on a farm

emergency sudden event that makes you act quickly

government people who make rules for a community, or the rules they make

lend let someone use something for a while before returning it

librarian person who works in a library

mobile home large trailer home that can be moved around but usually stays in one place

neighborhood small area of a city or town

patrol travel through an area to keep it safe

rodeo public show of special skills such as riding horses and roping cattle

town hall   building where a farm community's leaders meet

veterinarian   doctor who cares for animals

volunteer   person who offers to do a job, often without pay

More Books to Read

Caseley, Judith. *On the Town: A Community Adventure.* New York: Greenwillow, 2002.

Kalman, Bobbie. *What Is a Community?: from A to Z.* New York: Crabtree Publishing, 2000.

Kehoe, Stasia Ward. *I Live on a Farm.* New York: PowerKids Press, 1999.

Miller, Jake. *Who's Who in a Rural Community.* New York: PowerKids Press, 2005.

Turnbauer, Lisa. *Living in a Rural Area.* Mankato, Minn.: Capstone Press, 2005.

Index

animals 8, 12–13, 18, 25, 28–29

banks 22

business district 16

churches and temples 24

cities 4, 9, 13, 25, 27

emergency workers 15

farms and farmers 5-6, 8, 12-13, 18, 22, 26, 28

firefighters 15
food 18-19, 28–29

government 24

homes 6–7, 23

hospitals 25

libraries 20–21

neighborhoods 4–5

parks and play areas 10, 26-27
police 14
post offices 23

restaurants 13, 19
rodeos 29

schools 10–11
stores 7, 13, 16–17, 19

transportation 8–9

volunteers 15

work 8, 12–13